PRECISELY THAT
Reflections upon Enlightenment

Other Books by Rodney Stevens:

* *A Vastness All Around: Awakening to Your Natural State*

* *Fully Present: Daily Reflections on Nonduality*

* *State of Wonder: Awakening to Presence*

* *The Only True Life: Living from the Natural State*

Precisely That
Reflections upon Enlightenment

Rodney Stevens

"Just understand what you are, and carry on
your daily life to the best of your ability."

— *Sri Nisargadatta Maharaj*

CONTENTS

ACKNOWLEDGEMENTS

I want to thank Tim C. Taylor for his gracious and astute publishing assistance. It is a total pleasure to work with him, and I could not possibly have completed this book without him.

And my deepest appreciation to Lorna Fortis and the brothers Nishant and Purushottam Tyagi. Their benevolent words and ongoing donations have been such a tremendous help in this book getting published.

INTRODUCTION ~ THERE FOR THE SEEING

Rodney began writing these short, spontaneous compositions during the winter of 2014. Most were written on his MacBook Pro, while others were first composed in his coal-black notebook with which he always travels. Those entries were retyped onto Pages, his Mac's word processing program and then transferred to Rodney's much beloved 12-point Verdana font.

He completed the first draft a week before summer officially started— June 21. But the Southern swelter had already begun, and the book's revisions were made through the searing months of July and August. While most of the corrections and rewriting were made during Rodney's normal early morning writing hours, some of the editing was done after both an exhausting day at work and the humid trudge back to his apartment through triple-digit heat.

This is not a day-to-day journal of events, as he did in *Fully Present: Daily Reflections on Nonduality*. He makes no travels, other than to his dentist (for ongoing teeth and gum issues) and to his optometrist, for his annual eye exam and contact lens prescription. There are also no quixotic experiences here, no spiritual processes or mysterious ailments, other than his chronic insomnia, for which he now has medication. (How un-sagelike! Far better to suffer and to allow one's karma to play itself out, rather than polluting one's "spiritual plane" with some popular, prescriptive remedy!)

The essays are concise, poignant, and unfailingly pause-worthy. Reflect upon them, if you are drawn to do so. Neither faith nor belief is necessary in nonduality—a timeless teaching that directly points to your natural state of unchanging vastness. Feel these essays in your heart and being. Allow their pointing and intention to resonate within you, to pause you into a peace and spaciousness that is wholly beyond anything that you may have experienced before. Actually, you are that pause right now; it's there for the seeing, for the recognizing. Just a bit of alertness is all that is needed.

Indeed, you don't have to take a single step toward a single place or person for Self-knowledge. And why would you, given that you are the very thing that you are seeking? Mantras, spiritual journeys, guru adorations are part of the mystical trap into which false and deceptive teachers strive to ensnare gullible seekers, who are legion. Hope and pleading fill their eyes, as they trek to costly retreats, destinations, and gurus. None of that is necessary, of course. For you are presence itself! There is nothing to get and no place to go. No destiny, good works, or augury plays any part in this seeing, though providence and happenstance might. But why wait or hope for something that you are already?

A final point: When Rodney uses the words awareness and presence, he is pointing to the same thing. One word is just another way of using the other word, which, in turn, is just another way of pointing to that which is wholly beyond all measure and description. Indeed, it's laughable to think that a word or an expression can capture this inner immensity, which is both beginningless and eternal. So don't be excessively concerned when you see those expressions scattered throughout these pages. They are synonymous, and they are you.

ESSAYS

YOUR NATURAL STATE

There is no awakening, no enlightenment, or no liberation. You are what you are and have always been, which is perpetual awareness.

When you see or understand this, a profound presence of peace and spaciousness are suddenly there. You then comprehend how it has always been unequivocally *present*. It is so present, in fact, that sages sometimes call is presence itself. It has also been given the label of God, Brahman, Jehovah, the Creator, the Almighty, and countless other titles. Awareness, however, is totally beyond any name or description. No sect or religion is vast enough to contain it. Yet, in depicting it, perhaps nothing could be more accurate than the Biblical intimation: It is a "peace that passes all understanding." Nonetheless, this is your natural state. It is *what* you are at this very moment: Freedom itself.

PANCAKE HOUSE

You sit at your customary window table, watching bundled people scurrying passed. Pristine patches of lingering snow lay on the ground. Gunmetal clouds, with a heady mix of sleet and rain, threaten to cascade. You take another sip of your coffee, which is lukewarm now, but is not a problem.

Sarika, in whose section you always sit, will be bringing your waffle, three scrambled eggs, and grits in due course. In the meantime, she refills my cup and disappears. We've been doing this for years. She neither has to ask what I'm having or offer me a menu. I used to come here with a girlfriend. But no more. Couples sit snugly across the tables at one another. Some are talking, some aren't. You have never been here with someone who was smiling, focusing, *and* mirthful. One of those qualities was always missing. So now, your breakfasts are a solo affair.

But there no loneliness here. You gaze at the copy of the copy of a health and consciousness-centered weekly that you picked up at the nearby vitamin shop. The magazine lay unopened; you already know that much of it will be ho-hum and predictable—though spiritual seekers will likely find it a feast of nutritional and meditative matters.

Sleet begins to fall hard and crisply against the bare branches of the winter trees. The next bus won't be for another thirty minutes or so hour, and that's only if it is able to traverse the increasingly slippery highway. So there is no guessing when you will be home. Yet, you are waiting for nothing. Sarika refills your coffee cup. All is well.

NO UNDO EFFORT

Though I can't prove it, I suspect that such words as "reflection" and "contemplation" were changed (innocently or not) to "meditation" in such nondual scriptures as the *Upanishads* and *Brahma Sutras*. Or perhaps those three words are synonymous in Sanskrit. I don't know; for I'm neither a linguist or translator.

Why the concern? Meditation is an action towards the Self, and credible sages *and* the above teachings rightly declare that self-realization cannot occur that way. Reflection and deliberation are perfectly commendable ways to grasp nondual pointers, when done naturally—that is, when you are sitting or walking quietly, without any strain or undo effort. What are you to ponder? Among other things, that you are awareness itself. Even the "you" in the preceding sentence is something extra and is most certainly not anything concrete or perpetual. Muse too upon the fact that you never move from your fundamental nature. Appearances may say otherwise, but actuality, you do not. Even as you read these words, something is not altering in the least. What is that something?

SIGNIFIER OF THE ETERNAL

Mantras are groups of sounds composed by mostly anonymous savants, philosophers, and teachers. They point to Self in brief and often elegant ways (though my TM mantra was not the least bit melodious). Mantras are mainly for people who have a difficult time with the supposed abstract nature of nonduality.

Those words and expressions, it is said, should be gotten from a guru or teacher (or even paid for), less they will largely be ineffective. Why and how so? Clearly, that is a ridiculous supposition. The greatest mantra of all is entirely free and known by many: "Om." It is called the "eternal syllable" in the *Upanishads*, which are the last and philosophical portions of the *Vedas*. (It is in those portions that Advaita/nonduality texts are found.) The secret to Om (or to any mantra, actually) is not to emphasize the audible part of it. Directly after it is said, what is there? Or rather, what is not there? For a moment, there are no thoughts, beliefs, ideas, or sentiments—just a pause into the Eternal. In truth, the pause never leaves you. That is why you don't have to chant Om to get its power and stoppage—just *thinking* it is sufficient to experience that momentary cessation of mental chatter. That said, mantras are entirely unnecessary and are a wayward route to self-knowing.

NO SOVEREIGNTY

The bottom is line that you have misconstrued yourself to be the thinker, doer, and a perceiver. Thinking, action, and perceiving *are* going on, at least on an empirical, day-to-day level. The thinker and perceiver are notions arising and disappearing in your brain. The actions are there, but not the actor.

Having had this pointed out to you by a reliable source, you carefully, but naturally begin to question the solidity of your beliefs and ideas. A belief, by its very nature, has no substantialness, no sovereignty. For most of your life, you have assumed that the thinker (or even more incredibly, your body) to be your identity, your selfhood. In a word, the "who" of your life. There is no *who*, only a *what*. The "you" was never there. But that is no reason for fear or remorse, because *what* you are is greater than your mind could ever imagine! Yet, it is subtle, ordinary, and soundlessly spacious. This vastness is your fundamental reality and has simply gone unheeded.

GENIUS

Though *genius* (from the Latin "to beget") is a word that is used strange abandon these days, it usually typifies a person of exceptional creativity and insight. It's of little consequence whether the person produces little (logician Kurt Gödel and Zen master Tung Shan) or a lot (Bach and Shakespeare).

Einstein said "Everyone is a genius." But I think it would be more accurate to say that everyone has genius within them. For some people, that aptitude will show in mathematics and design; while in others, it will flourish in writing and teaching. The form and capacity are irrelevant. Further, an authentic genius takes an area or topic and makes it his own. He brings depth and numinousity to every new reading, listening, or pondering. (Ironically, the person may or may not have an astronomical IQ!) We see ample evidence of such brilliance when we think of Thomas Aquinas skillfully dictating to multiple scribes at once and having the acumen to declare that God is *"esse ipsum"* ("Being itself"), Nisagardatta Maharaj bringing verve and nuance to his discussions with spiritual seekers from the world over, and U.G. Krishnamurti's volatile directives to questioners' presumptive "I's" and "Me's" (though yes, he raged too mightily at times). And what of the venerable but little-known Gaudapauda (c.500 C.E.) and Lao Tzu (Sixth c. B.C.E.) who cleverly chastised the renown Confucius about his rules of behavior, saying, "Why these flags of benevolence and righteousness so bravely upraised, as though you were beating a drum and searching for a lost child?" Brilliant beings all.

ABOUNDINGLY PRESENT

You can't reach what you already are. So any idea of acquiring or attainment has to be seen through. Otherwise, you will be chasing a stereotypical notion of "enlightenment" that will bring you not a millionth of an inch closer to what you are seeking.

There are no visions, specters, or soulful expansions to experience—just an easy discernment of your natural and everyday state, which you will discover to be deep peace and spaciousness. I suppose you could call this a revelation, of sorts; but that seems too blaring an appraisal. For the hushness of all of this is totally without parallel. And with this recognition comes the understanding that the hushness is *you*, that you are not your mind, name, personality, or form. Some lingering self-identification may need to be seen through; but it is no big deal. Indeed, to unnecessarily dwell on that point is simply the "Me" in subtle operation again!

BIG BANG

Scientists, using special telescopes at the South Pole in Antarctica, have discovered primordial gravitational waves created approximately 13.8 billion years ago, near the moment when the universe came into being.

These waves, say the scientists, were created "a trillionth of a trillionth of a trillionth of a second" after the Big Bang itself, when the universe was roughly the size of the nail on your pinky finger! The kid and science lover in me find all of this enthralling, given the tremendous energies and monumental forces (physical and subatomic) at play during those first few moments. I continue to peruse any developing stories and updates on the Web and in the papers. But how and why those wrenching forces came into being holds no real interest to me; indeed, I suspect that we will never know the "why" and the "how"—and that's perfectly okay. Ancient and realized nondual philosophers have rightly said that awareness is "birthless." The universe, however extraordinary and seemingly-endless, is just another appearance of space and form. How it all began is just humdrum speculation, to my mind. Moreover, right here and now, you are entirely beyond the universe and the Big Bang themselves! Now *that* is truly riveting.

EVER ABIDING

What is nonduality? My cursory, West-coast response is that, "It is an all-is-oneness kind of thing." Surprisingly, the answer works, giving people a kind of intuitive feel of what is being pointed to, even though the description sounds a bit "out there" and is in no way practical or attainable.

A more precise rendering would probably be: "It is a deep and straightforward inquiry into your natural state." You engage in a reflective probing, of sorts, that is neither time-dependent or action-oriented. You can either take note of the things that are changing (your body, thoughts, and states of consciousness) or you can focus on whatever it is that isn't altering in the least. (And there is only one thing that is doing that!) You can also come to this understanding through logic and insight, providing you see where the reasoning and discernments are pointing. Some ancient teachers have said that the nondual scriptures are the final authority themselves. But they aren't. You are. Your own direct and personal experience of your abiding state is both the answer and the mandate. Stay clear on the point, and you won't get distracted by any well-intentioned spiritual fluff.

SANS MUSE

Inspiration: I'm sure it happens, but I don't require it. Daily, ordinary, events are my muses—no mystifying daemons or tutelary spirits needed here.

I would be just as "inspired" in Oxford, Mississippi (with its sweltering summers, famed Square Books bookstore, Faulknerian milieu, and bountiful Southern breakfasts) as I would in Oxford, England (with its striking collegiate quadrangles, Port Meadow expanses, and shop-ladened High Street at Radcliffe Square). My schedule would be the same as it is now—getting up between around 4:00am, making coffee, and going to my MacBook Pro to write, respond to emails, schedule phone consultations, and do more writing. On the five days a week that I go to my job, I still get up at the same time, but I stop writing at 6:30 to clock-in at 7:00am. I work to pay the bills. Fortunately, my job is not an especially difficult—I'm a security officer at a large mall. Presence is a felt and living reality for me, whether I'm writing or patrolling. Thus, I am alert to creative stimuli that is constantly presenting itself to this body and mind, as well as to the vastness that is behind and beyond all of that.

WHO IS THE KNOWER?

Is there a more vital question about inquiry than this? It has a visceral rightness to it, like falling in love or strolling along a seashore or gasping at a range of powder blue mountains. Any of those will pause your thinking.

And thinking has to be slowed in order for you to perceive the boundlessness surrounding all thoughts and feelings; and note that I said "slowed," not stopped. You can no more stop your mentation than you can swim to the moon. Thinking is part of your biological and neurological framework. It is a process, a response to your environment that allows you to, among other things, react properly to stimuli, as well as to smoothly convey information and feelings to others. So go ahead, live your life as normally and as compassionately as possible. But don't bother striving for some kind of veiled Keatsian calmness; for that can be so easily disturbed. Presence, however, is unalterable—and it is that in which emotions and feelings arise and disappear. You are the knower, not anything that arises in it.

That Which Is

Can you remain with what currently is? Not with the events or occurrences at the moment, but with what you are existing *as* right now, as an unchanging *presence* of awareness. This recognition takes only a moment. And I'm not speaking of some strained merging with anything, just a simple cognizance of what is always consummately present.

What is existent is awareness, of course. There also appears to be—working our way backwards, according to classic Upanishadic writers—your Body, Breath, Mind (memory, feelings, etc), Intelligence (reasoning, creativity, etc), and Bliss (conditioned happiness, such as receiving something that you've always wanted or profoundly loving someone). If you notice, each one of these appearances becomes finer and finer, but no less moving. Yet, they are all functions and appearances, and therefore temporary and changeable. There is, however, something that is perfectly beyond those so-called five "coverings" of the Self. What is that something? You can *say* that it is awareness all day long. But you have to see it for yourself. Go to where these words are pointing. You don't have to make a single step. Not one.

INTIMACY OF THE SETTING

Upanishad is such a beautiful word. Etymologists tell us that it means or indicates "sitting down near," an expression which is as arresting as the word itself. This, literally, was the way that spiritual instruction was given to seekers in early India.

But today we have phone calls, Skype calls, and video conferencing. It is more than a little amazing that my Skype consultations can pretty much be done with anyone around the world with a computer and an internet connection. There is, of course, something to be said for sitting and talking personally with someone or to a small group. It offers an easy intimacy, fellowship, and the spontaneous arising of fruitful and pause-worthy moments. Those same moments can occur with Skype and video calls, as well, if the teacher has a living understanding of his or her actual nature. But whether they are felt, heard, or noticed is largely dependent upon the questioner. So much is being said, hinted at, and pointed to when a credible source is responding to your queries. Please know, however, that it is your very own stillness arising in those moments. The teacher is transferring nothing!

BLISSLESS AT STARBUCKS

You sit at one of the tiny, rear tables at Starbucks, with your "tall" Vanilla blond roast and half-eaten glazed doughnut before you. People come and go, mostly women, barelegged and in heels or sandals—their pale feet so pretty in the morning coolness, a coolness that gives no presage of the coming swelter (98F today, with a heat index of 104-degrees).

Customers are getting their Caffè Lattes and White Chocolate Mochas to go, which is good, because there are no available seats in the smallish but winsome space. You have never met or talked with anyone here. This has always been one of your solitary places. As ever, your *New York Times* has been separated into its sections: National, Business, the Arts, and Science Times. You could easily put down the paper and sit here for most of the day, not moving in the least—except for the occasional trip to the restroom. There would be neither the effort to sit nor the attempt to gain some manufactured calmness. Your eyes would be half-closed naturally, because you find them restful in that position when you are simply sitting like this. There are no stereotypical "bliss" here to which seekers can aspire; but rather, something immensely better: A hushed and unwavering serenity pervading the whole of your body and mind. So not moving is one of the easiest things to do. No shift into anything is required here. You are simply sitting with this vastness and beauty, you own true Self. But you don't want to appear bizarre or catatonic. So you return to your paper, nibble at your doughnut, and sip your sumptuous coffee—though you miss your vanilla caramel creamer that you always use at home. No matter. All is well.

THAT SOUNDLESS MELODY

Om is the music I hear as I type these words. It isn't so much music as it is a soundless, one-note melody. It neither changes nor intensifies, and it appears to be coming from both nowhere and everywhere. It's little wonder that Om is found in all the Upanishads (the Advaitic/nondual portions of the Vedas) and is said, by sages and Sanskrit experts alike, to comprise *all* words, sounds, mantras, and all languages.

Why this cosmic utterance presents itself, I do not know. I did notice it immediately after coming to this understanding. Perhaps it was there the entire time, merely being overlooked. This ancient mantra and mystical sound is usually inscribed as:

When written in Devanagari script (as above), it is particularly sublime, with its echoing loops proffering elegant intimations of the numinous. Its definitions range from the "name of God" to the "primordial sound at the creation of the universe." Which is correct (and perhaps they both are!) really doesn't matter. For me, Om is a vibration that presents itself throughout this body/mind appearance and is a timeless signifier of awareness itself. Yes, Om too is an appearance—but what a grand, subtle, and pause-worthy one! For it sings of nothing but the Ultimate. And what could be more wonderful than that?

No Water, No Moon

I scan one of the spiritual magazines in a bookstore. This rarely happens; for I know that, in all likelihood, the magazine will quickly bore me or that I will start to scowl or laugh at some thoroughly ridiculous article (e.g., "No Shortcut to Awakening," "Practicing Pure Awareness," "Commune with Your Higher Spirit," "Enlightenment: Culmination of Years of Effort").

In this Buddhist publication, I come across a piece about enlightened women. The authors could only come up with three of them, with the most recent being from 13th century Japan—the famous and beautiful Chiyono, of the "no water, no moon tale" Zen story. Her sudden realization (which appears authentic) was precisely that—Zen-like. She became self-realized *after* trying every meditative, devotional, ritualistic, and Buddhistic approach that she could find. "She studied for years," the tale says. But no method work for her—not one! Then one night, while struggling with a pail of water, the bamboo strips that held the pail burst. Suddenly, there was no more water and no more appearances of the moon *in* the water. This paused her significantly and thoroughly. Indeed, there was no more Chiyono—just the vastness of her own true Self.

CATEGORICALLY PRESENT

The seer cannot be the seen. So anything that can be touched, tasted, heard, or observed cannot possibly be you. Now, where does that leave you—literally?

Your body, thoughts, and emotions can immediately be ruled out, because they are appearances that can be viewed or witnessed. Ditto your personality, changing states of consciousness, and intricately functioning nervous system. (Though the latter is probably closer to the mark than the previous items!) So the query becomes: What is it that is fully present but no qualities or aspects? The question can't be answered by the mind because a thought is just another appearance. But when mental chatter is naturally and temporarily halted, the solution to the question is easily found. For the space within the halting *is* the answer! Again, what is it that is fully present but cannot be observed? Stay with the question, if you are so inclined, until a serene and unchanging spaciousness is directly perceived and felt. *That* is who and what you are. It is not an object because, among other things, it never changes, and it never comes and goes. It is simply what it is and what will always be.

PROLIFIC AND SAINTLY

While growing up, I was always moved by Albrecht Dürer's 1514 engraving of *Saint Jerome in His Study*. I remember first coming across this work as an adolescent, while perusing my set of *World Book Encyclopedias* and being immediately taken with St. Jerome's fervor, concentration, and obvious beatitude.

Only later in life did I read about the great intricacy within the etching, including the hypnotic shadows; the contemplative ambience; the thick, richly patterned windows that helps to keep one's focus within the study; and the dried gourds hanging from the rafters, symbolizing courage in the face of theological controversy. Saint Jerome's incessant literary activity (he was the second most prolific writer of Latin Christianity—with Saint Augustine being the first) included translations of Greek authors, original commentaries on the Old Testament, New Testament commentaries, and his fervid epistles. Coming across his picture now on the Web, I smile, still marveling at his literary industry, but I'm deeply aware of his roundabout way to the numinous.

ATTENTIVENESS

Can you really listen to someone without thoughts during a conversation? Why would you even want to do that, as some New Age spiritualists would have you do? Don't you want to be able to reply clearly and intelligibly to what is being said or asked?

Thoughts pause on their own during a conversation, particularly when something beautiful or significant is being said or discerned. Then mentation reappears, in response to what has been heard or witnessed. The thoughts may or may not be an accurate reflection of events. Nonetheless, they are naturally there, assisting you in communicating with others and in gauging the state of your immediate environment. It's ludicrous when teachers direct seekers behave and listen like some etheric automaton. Given that the teachers are not self-realized themselves, they have a vapid and clichéd view about how it is to live an "enlightened" life. So choose your spiritual mentors very carefully. Be attentive to what *they* have come to know and understand—or the lack thereof!

THE NATURAL STATE

To speak about this is one of the simplest things. The words flourish of their own accord, as if you were watching some faintly familiar person verbalize about this recognition from the perspective of your own head. And there appears to be no end to what "this person" could say about the subject!

Yet, you go for nearly a week without saying anything to anyone about at it at all. Then your two-days off from work arrive, and you find yourself squeezing in phone and video discussions with people from diverse corners of the world. With coffee or water at hand, you rattle on throughout the day, until your voice is raspy. For the rest of the week, silence about the Silence. And since you live alone, you are quiet most of the time anyway—even when Bach or R&B is blaring from the radio or the CD player. There is the writing too, of course—the books and blog, as well as profusion emails to attend to. There are a few things that would make all of this much easier; however, you do what you can with what you have. And in this *lived* life, grace abounds.

A SIMPLE STORY

This anecdote has been recounted in Advaitic and nondual circles for many years, though I first heard it in the 1980s. A seeker arrived at an ashram and was told that he may have to serve the guru for twelve years if he wanted to attain enlightenment. The seeker hardily agreed. He chanted mantras, meditated for hours, ate only vegetarian foods, and experienced numerous ecstatic states.

When he would see the guru each day, he would drop to his knees in extraordinary reverence. The guru, amused each time he did this, would softly say to him "Thou art that" and strove off.

After a dozen exhausting years had passed, the seeker still hadn't discovered his true Self. So he packed his bags and went to see another guru in a neighboring village.

Once there, he carefully explained to the other teacher how he had devotedly served the first guru for twelve years and still had not found awareness. The guru paused, gazed at him for a few moments, and then softly uttered, "Thou art that." The seeker instantly saw what *both* gurus was pointing to—his natural state. It was the same message, but for whatever reason, he heard the words freshly, in a totally different way.

EASE OF SEEING

Self-knowing isn't taxing. Where is the difficulty? Who is it that isn't seeing what is being said? And who is this "who" that keeps rising and disappearing?

If you remain with these questions (in a natural and reflective manner), the answers will likely reveal themselves in short order. Additionally, the revelation will be a living understanding of who and what your actual identity is, i.e., unchanging peace and spaciousness. There is no path to this; no prayer or petitioning will assist you here—for the simple reason that you are awareness itself! You just aren't seeing that that is the reality, that that has already happened. Actually, it didn't even happen! It was always the case. So as you are reading these words on this ordinary day or evening, you are greater than you could ever imagine. Even the universe pales in comparison to your timeless existence. All the scriptures are pointing to what you are, right here and now. See the enormity that! See that there is nothing to do except perceive the truth of your very own presence.

AN INNER SOLICITUDE

Without self-knowledge, life is bound to be challenging and stressful. Have you ever wondered why this is so? Perhaps there is some underlying cause that you have yet to fathom.

And there is, course: An unfamiliarity with your genuine nature (that you are presence and not your body, mind, and personality) leads to unexamined desires; this, in turn, creates destructive and unwholesome actions. With self-knowledge, you continue to have desires and inclinations—you just are no longer attached to them. You also clearly discern how none of these impulses (a more neutral term) truly stick around. They are there one moment, and gone the next. If some momentary attachment does occur, it's of little consequence and is easily dealt with. For you now have a natural proclivity towards fairness, compassion, and goodwill. You aren't abiding by some strict and specific moral code. That disposition is simply there.

Shankara's Response

When asked what is the greatest obstacle to liberation, Shankara said "laziness." I strongly disagree. For most spiritual seekers are not lazy at all. In truth, they are engaged in multitudes of practices with full abandon! And some of those practices are extremely arduous.

The central impediment to self-realization is an over-complication of it. For there is really nothing to do, except see or understand that you are awareness proper. It is because of that simplicity that self-knowing appears to be either some distant abstraction or something for the "chosen few." Mantras, meditation, mindfulness, and devotion are all activities of the mind. Each has to do with attainment and reaching. Also, they are all time-related. If you want to do them for their own enjoyment or for whatever health-benefits they may offer, please do. That's perfectly fine. Just know that presence isn't arrived at that way. It is only discerned.

GOOD FRIDAY RAIN

You stand on your balcony, gazing into the frigid, Good Friday rain. The temperature is in the mid-40s, but it feels much colder; afternoon traffic is heavy with people either headed home or to Easter weekend outing or vacation.

The dull popping of the rain upon the magnolia leaves is music to your ears. The tree is directly in front of you, and slightly to the left. If you stand on my tiptoe, you can almost touch the tree's crown. Though you are dressed in a sweater and T-shirt, you cross your arms against the dampness and cold. Occasional spatters from the shower can be felt on your hands, face, and stocking feet. You could easily step back inside to the light and warmth of your tiny apartment. But there is a sacredness here, on this raw, raucous, bustling afternoon. There is also a silence, despite the pronounced *pocking* of the rain against the magnolia fronds. You begin to shiver. Involuntarily, you tighten your arms across your chest against the cold and wetness. Yet, you are beyond fulfilled.

Attainment

Kindness, generosity, and cultivating the mind will not bring you to this understanding. All of that has to be halted (in a natural and non-deterministic manner) to see your own true Self.

Seekers think that some action is required for "enlightenment." But you can't trade one thing for something else in nonduality. One endeavor is analogous to another. No deed can take you to self-knowledge, except the recognition that no action is required. You are presence at this very moment; therefore, you are timeless, formless, and unborn—a single unitary package of Oneness. Because you are identifying with, among other things, your body, feelings, and personality, you think that that oneness isn't there. You think that you have to search for it or to beseech some saint or heavenly host for awareness to be bestowed upon you. But presence is fully present! Simply see that that is the case. Don't look at the word to grasp this; but rather, note what is already *existing* after reading the word. The word is no more the thing than a map is the territory.

SO WHERE IS THE WORRY?

Before becoming self-realized, I noticed an extrasensory perception periodically occurring within me. It continues to appear, though not as much. I watch it, with minimum curiosity, I assure you.

It is a kind of clairvoyance, I suppose, and that's all I care to say about it. I suspect it can be fine-tuned and utilized, though I have no interest in doing so. On the other hand, I am not attempting to halt it either. When it happens, fine; and when it does not, that's perfectly okay too. There is just a calm neutrality about its appearance. Yet, I can't smiling when something flashes in my head, and it turns out to be true. If that aspect of this body/mind disappears tomorrow, I would not be bothered in the least. In-the-Least! I *cannot*, however, say that about presence. But then, now I see how it can clearly never be lost.

Disenthrallment

This is what it feels like to have this understanding: No center, no periphery. Yes, the body is there, but it is just another appearance in the vastness.

Thoughts, feelings, recollections, and even conditioned responses come and go, but with only a modicum of interest here. This applies to joy and happiness, as well, of course. Why? Because if you give partiality to them, you will likely be overly reactive to sorrow. That just doesn't happen here. But fret not, this disinterest to emotions won't turn you into an emotionless droid; there will still be smiles, laughter, tears, and celebration. There just won't be any bonding with them. A final note: This impartiality can only be made from the perspective of presence. The mind cannot do this; for it is partially itself! Neither can any effort, strictures, or avoidances deliver you to this non-attachment, because, at bottom, all of those are just the actions of the mind.

YOUR OWN TRUE SELF

Genius can take numerous forms: High IQ, profuseness, great learning, artistry (painting, photography, graphic design, etc), great abilities (athletic, musical, etc), and singular skills (writing, speaking, teaching, conversing, practicing medicine, etc).

True genius is at once atypical and ordinary. There is nothing really freakish about him or her. If you were to have coffee or tea with the person, it would seem one of the most natural things. Yet, the conversation would be made wondrous by the person's inspiring presence and spontaneous revelations. Further, there would be no angst to her artistry—just a joyful doing in whatever her work may be, as well as unceasing innovation. Prime examples of all the above is Matthew Carter, designer of the elegant Verdana typeface for computer screens; Jean-Pierre Kaplan, producer of the sleeping aid, Ambien; Lee Child, prolific and adroit creator of the Jack Reacher novels; and Daniele Bovet, the Swiss-born Nobel Prize-winning pharmacologist who not only discovered the first antihistamine, but developed important muscle-relaxing drugs that are used in surgery today. Bovet never bothered to get patents for many of his creations, patents that would have easily made him a very wealthy man!

STILLNESS

I sit at a comfortable melanic table. Overhead, a burly, Starbucks, umbrella protects from the morning sun. Fronting my table are green hedges, chrysanthemum bushes (garlanded with tiny vermillion blossoms) and a snug array of yellow-blotch pansies.

Mouthwatering aromas emanate from the store every time someone goes in or out the doors. People are indeed coming and going, whether to have breakfast, meet someone, or enjoy some caffeinated brew inside. But I am waiting for nothing and no one—just enjoying the coolish morning. Shortly, I'll be heading to the Original Pancake House a few doors up. I like to stop here for an added bit of sitting and stillness, as well as to pick up a *New York Times* before going to the Pancake House. I've never been much of a people-watcher—especially when it comes to attractive women, from whom I purposely look away. They get enough stares from other men (and women!) without mine being added to the mix. But I needn't be concerned: Ninety percent of them are on cell phones and oblivious, it seems, to their surroundings. They all are so busy and in a bustle. Everyone is. No stillness anywhere.

WHERE THE GREATNESS LIES

The Bengali poet and philosopher Rabindranath Tagore (1861-1941) said "the aim of a true work of art is to give a form to what escapes definition." That's close to the mark. Instead of "definition," I would use "assessment" or "evaluation." Yes, such works are great, as well. But we are at a lost to say precisely where the greatness lies and why it is so. We could point to this and that, but after a while, we simply find ourselves being quiet.

Such creations that come to mind are Johann Sebastian Bach's music, U.G. Krishnamurti's early talks (which were largely absent of tirades and censure), Derek Walcott's poems, the *Upanishads* (by various anonymous writers), Nisargadatta's satsangs, some of the Buddha's recorded sayings in *The Diamond Vehicle*, Magnus Carlsen's chess playing, and Dante's *Divine Comedy*. Interesting note about the latter: In a missive to his patron (Can Grande Della Scala), Dante said his central goal in writing this epic poem was to bring readers to "the state of bliss." He does nearly that in some of his polished and multilayered passages from "Purgatory" and "Paradise." Still, your natural state is completely beyond any euphoria that may momentarily be had by reading this masterly work.

Self-Knowledge

You can come to this understanding in primarily two ways: By directly recognizing your natural state or by reflecting upon the unmissable evidence that everything around you (your body, mind, states of consciousness, nature, people, the universe, etc) is in a state of flux.

One approach is not better than the other. It depends upon your temperament and personality. This is neither a process nor a method; that would make them time-laden and would intimate that there is something "out there" to procure. Your immensity exists right now, as your ordinary, everyday awareness. There is nothing to do, except take note that this is what you are and that there was never a time in which you were without it.

CONTRITION

Where did I come across the beautiful quote from the 16th-century French writer St. Francis de Sales, who wrote that "even our repentance must be peaceful"? There are few (if any) "shoulds" and "musts" in the spiritual life; but Sales' suggestion is a fine one.

Yet, "Who" would be repenting? It would only be a thought or a memory of a previous thought (or action). The supposed "sin" has come and gone; it was just an action, feeling, or desire that was *labeled* sinful by the mind. So neither the sin nor the sinner is truly there. They are products of thought and imagination. (We are not discussing murder or crimes of passion here. Various societies and regions of the world have different statutes. If you live in a specific country, it is incumbent upon you to obey its laws.)

Wouldn't it be far better to heed John 3:7, when he says (in the often elegant English Revised Version of the Bible), "Marvel not that I said unto thee, Ye must be born anew"? And note: That final adverb is not "again," but *anew*. Nothing is transformed, made better, or even born! There is merely the recognition of something that is perpetually present. It *appears* to be produced because of one's newfound serenity and boundlessness. Presence is at once old and new, and hence eternal. But it can only be pointed to, and of course, experienced.

Daily Life

Day after day, year after year, people go about their lives with all the drama, boredom, tension, and moments of pleasure. But to whom does these things appear? If the spiritually inquisitive were to remain with that question, they would likely discover its answer, an answer that would be ever-present and ever-immaculate.

In truth, there is a deep inclination within us to raise the question, in some shape, form, or manner. No doubt it is because we are presence itself. In some people, the urge for self-discovery is faint. In my case, it was indomitable. But don't use me as an example or a template. For everyone comes to this apprehension differently, though the "mechanics" (such a lamentable word choice) are pretty much the same: A pause into Beingness, into your own natural and palatial state. Given that, there needn't be any waiting or hoping for anything. Indeed, *who* would be waiting? And *why* even hope for self-knowledge when you are presence itself? Again, awareness is precisely what you are! There is no *who*! That is the understanding! There is no *who*—only unbounded capaciousness.

NO ATTRIBUTES

How can you not be awareness? Feel the pause of that inquiry. Don't mentally search for an answer; for the mind will not be able to provide you with one, however much it may try. Again, how can you not be awareness?

If you quietly remain with the question, the answer will be there, in all of its glory and timelessness. It doesn't come into being or is somehow made active! True existence never alters from what it is, and it is nothing less than what you are right now. However, it wouldn't be correct to say that your natural state is pure awareness; the latter has no attributes whatsoever and is not even aware of itself! But when presence radiates through our mind/body appearances, Self-knowing is possible, and we are directly able to know and understand that we are presence itself, and not what we appear to be—that is, our thoughts, emotions, and personality. Sadly, many seekers define themselves by the number and variety of experiences they have had. Self-knowledge figures not at all into their mystical and paranormal rubrics.

IT HAS NO NAME

All there is, is awareness. And you *are* that awareness. So how can there be any relationship between you and thoughts? Or between you and your body, intelligence, personality, or even your bank account?

All of those things are just temporary arisings in presence. Yes, they have a day-to-day reality and practicality. Fundamentally, though, you are greater than all of that. Come back to what you are, to that eternal vastness that has no name. What is the way? There is none, except to recognize that you were never not precisely that—the Absolute, which exceeds all forms, labels, attributes, and even spirituality! Despite all appearances, you beyond time, space, and dogma, which are nothing but concepts. You are that which has no name. What is that? Something is present that has no name. Come back to this. See its reality and presence. That is what you are! That is what the sages and the Vedas were pointing to—an eternal *whatness*. Truly, this is your Reality. You never move from this.

INTERLUDE

The interval between two thoughts or throughout deep sleep are all the same thing: Pristine awareness. This isn't a void or some "mere nothingness" (as many Buddhists believe) because neither of those things can produce the quality of knowingness and tranquility in our mind/body forms. Awareness, however, does precisely this once it is realized.

I emphasize pauses because they are easy to take note of. They are there between any two notions, ideas, and memories. As for deep sleep, consciousness (your sense of an individual self) is not active (which tells you that consciousness too is an appearance). Also, your body is getting deep rest at this time, which is imperative to its health and functioning. Thus, the time to alert to pauses is during your normal waking hours. These moments can be especially potent when you are conversing with a self-realized teacher or reading his or her words. Or when you are simply having a cup of tea or coffee in a quiet, reflective manner. You are not attempting to be paused; but rather, to be alert to the profound and inherent peace *within* the pauses when they spontaneously occur.

ORIGINALITY

Creativity is not found just in long and nuanced projects. It flourishes in succinct and incidental endeavors, as well, such as calligraphy, micro fiction and essays, flower arranging, and discussions, such as the potent and soul-opening conversations that Nisargadatta had with spiritual seekers from the world over.

They have been many occasions, with this writer, when a question or problem was stubbornly present. Then, a few hours later (or a day, at most), the solution was there. During those occasions, there is no "me" working on the issue. Yet, it got resolved with winning and spontaneous originality, which appears to come from some place "outside" of any constricted creator. Remember, originality isn't necessarily something new; but rather, something profound, elemental, and pause-worthy. It has its roots simultaneously in the everyday and the extraordinary.

TRUE SELF

You are neither the body nor the mind. Usually that pointer is written as: "You are neither your body nor your mind." Do you see how much more powerful it is without the adjective "your"?

You are the spaciousness in which the body and mind arise. With just a little vigilance, you can effortlessly see that that spaciousness is directly there. In truth, it is the *only* thing that is both not changing and is continually present. There is nothing else in your field of perception about which you can say that. Nothing! So this *knowingness* has to be the Self, Presence, Awareness, Brahman, God, Allah, or Supreme Light about which the *rishis* and spiritual texts have pointed. It doesn't matter what you call or designate it. The key issue is that you recognize that you *are* it. So come back to the previously mentioned pointer: You are neither the body nor the mind. Allow these words to easily direct you to what you actually are. Nothing, I assure you, could be simpler.

WONDERFULLY PRESENT

We can only know what we already are. So self-understanding is a matter of discerning what is currently present. You don't have to wait for it, attain it, or hope that it will make some future appearance. It is within and before you at this very instant.

Further, you are presence precisely. This understanding occurs only if you remain clear of the conceptual and the psychological—for awareness is neither of the mind or the body. Neither is there anything transcendental about it. And who would be doing the "transcending" anyway? So with nothing to get and nowhere to go, you are left, yet again, with your own Self—your natural and unmoving state, which is merely being neglected, bypassed, and given short shrift. When it comes to Self-knowledge, the question is not how can I reach this grandness, but rather, what is it that is before and within me that is not being perceived? The great writer Johann Wolfgang von Goethe was one-hundred percent correct when he said, "The hardest thing to see is what is in front of your eyes." And presence could not be more immediately before you!

SOURCE OF SPLENDOR

When you are experiencing joy, happiness, or love, it appears to be coming from the object, occurrence, or person. But it isn't, at least not wholly so. There is also a deep and underlying peace within each situation; however, because you are focusing on the object or individual, you are missing the source of your splendor.

Ordinary emotions cannot be sustained. But you want precisely that for your object, situation, or lover. Eventually, you'll find that the joy for the person or circumstance lessens, and that you bright new love becomes familiar. That needn't be the case; for on all of those occasions, you are privy to presence, which neither moderates or becomes commonplace. When you see the *source* from which the entity, circumstance, or person radiates, you cherish them for themselves. There is no clinging to them. It's a simple kind of non-attachment that is both welcoming and ever-new. That is the essence of true love.

A NATURAL QUIETNESS

When you are in the company of someone who has perceived his natural state, you can't help feeling a certain quietness with that person, even if he or she is animated and gregarious. The realized person (a woefully inaccurate expression!) fully feels that silence and hushness within himself, of course.

The moment the conversation begins, that peacefulness—more often not—pervades the speaker's words, with little or no attempt by the speaker to do anything. It simply happens, a flowing forth of stillness and presence, as naturally as the words themselves. Allow yourself to feel this completely. Don't strain to "get" anything; for the moment you attempt to grasp or seize this, it's gone, like an apparition and phantasmagoria. Merely see that this felt presence is happening on its own. It may appear to be sporadic, but it isn't. It is unequivocally there, all the time and in every place. Truly, there is nothing *more* there than this!

YOU ARE THE ANSWER

Self-knowing is simply a matter of seeing what is presenting itself—not to you, but *as* you. It is no more or less than that. Overly exploring various definitions and parsing classic nondual texts are merely ways of avoiding any real grasping of oneself.

Don't attempt to force an answer, for you *are* the answer—your own perpetual state of deep peace and spaciousness. Attuning yourself to its presence is a one-time nonevent: You instantly discover that it is there. And once seen, it is always perceived. There may be some fine-tuning here and there, but it won't have anything to do with greater or lasting bliss. It will likely be any linger episodes of self-identification with thoughts and reactions. Then again, there may be none of that. In either case, they are easily dealt with by the solid understanding what you are and have always been—unequivocal awareness.

THE MOST IMPORTANT THING

Though seekers make much to do about reigning in desires, attachment, and the ego, you can't do so from the perspective of the mind, because all of those things are just other thoughts! The mind is nothing but the appearance of a thought. A higher intelligence is needed for this apprehension, and that is precisely what presence is.

Ironically, the most important of the psychological aspects listed above is not the ego or desires, but attachment. For if you have no long-term bond with your inclinations or the ego, where is the problem? (Providing there is no harm to the person or to others.) Also, true non-attachment can only come after self-realization. Why? Because you are then seeing thoughts, feelings, and yearnings for what they are—momentary impetuses are in awareness. You categorically know that you are awareness and not anything appearing within it, no matter how glorious, fetching, or pleasurable. Non-attachment has to be resolved (through seeing and understanding, and not by any spiritual or intellectual posturing). Otherwise, psychological suffering will continue.

RECOGNITION

Awakening is the spontaneous recognition of your natural state. There is nothing you can do to progressively attain or "reach" this perception. Awareness, after all, is your nature, your underlying condition. That's why "awakening" is not a choice term for this *Knowingness*. It is used here and elsewhere in the book because it is what most people know and understand.

But we shouldn't get too concerned with terms and expressions, either. For we are pointing to something that is perfectly present. Do you see the loveliness and simplicity of that? We are speaking about something that you currently and categorically *are*. There is nothing to reach and nowhere to go because you are presence itself. So the question becomes, "What is it that I am missing? ...What is it, right here and now, that is not being seen? ...What is it that is absolutely within and before me, but is not being perceived?" Allow these inquiries to saturate your being; live with them throughout the day and evening, in an easy and engaging manner. Don't force anything! No exertion or bullying tactics are needed in nonduality. Indeed, they are countermeasures to your success, which is the full-seeing of your unremitting vastness.

Query

"Who am I?"

The answer is already present before you can reply to the question; it is *what* you are at any given moment. So though the question is a vital one, it truly lags with its proximity to awareness! In fact, there is no relationship between the questioner and presence, because all there is, is awareness. The question and questioner are all conceptual, mere appearances in an underlying Reality. Understand this, and you will spontaneously fathom the immediacy of your enduring Self. The question is solely a pointer; don't take it too seriously. And most certainly don't turn it into an abstraction or some mental or verbal repetition—or even worse, a spiritual posture by which others can see how devoted, singular, and meditative you are.

NO MORE

You relax on one of the outdoor sofas in front of Starbucks. It's a warm, spring day, with the temperature in the low 90's. The sidewalk is shaded by the store's expansive awning. Propitious breezes continue to refresh—this, along with the penetrating serenity that abounds within you.

A young man in his 20's is perched on a neighboring sofa. He's dressed in casual black, so he could easily be one of the baristas from inside. He wears brightly colored earbuds connected to an iPod, which lolls in his lap, and sits crossed-legged with his back perfectly straight. His hands are in a semi-relaxed mudra, and his head is nodding. He appears to be listening to some kind of meditative music. But he's quiet; he neither hums nor disturbs. There is some spiritual book next to him, but it is facing down, with the title hidden. Years ago, you might have gone over (after he had finished), casually and graciously introduced yourself, and—if you found him to be a serious seeker—quietly uttered, "Perhaps I can help you with all of that." But no more. It seems to frighten people, to have this tall, skinny, black guy come over to them and declare, "That this thing for which you are searching has happened to me, and that it is indeed a peace that passes all understanding. Would you like to talk about it?" But you would immediately see the nervousness in their eyes, as if you were something foreboding and to be hurried from. How could someone as ordinary-looking as this guy be awakened? So you never approach anyone any more. Ever.

REFLECT UPON THESE THINGS

Just sitting with this understanding is more beautiful and serene than any yoga pose could ever possibly be.

Please continue to perform your yoga or meditation, if you relish doing them. Enjoy them for what they are and do them without any stress or desire for achievement. And here is a yoga pointer from a former yoga teacher (me): To sit fully and comfortably in one position is to sit in them all. For the Self is there in each and very asana. One is no closer to presence than another. Generally, the moment you attempt to seek the Self through strenuous and painful practice, you "loose" it because your focus is on the pain and the "getting." So reflect upon these things, in an easy and heartfelt manner. For when it comes to Self-knowing, there really isn't anything to be done—only discovered.

THE REFINED

The ancient Advaitic and nondual scriptures describe those who have awakened as "knowers of the subtle."

I love that expression. For it seamlessly points to the fact that awareness, when manifested through our bodies and minds, is a hushed and beauteous ubiquity. Yet, it is so easily overlooked. So what is a seeker to do? Keep coming back to the actuality that what you are searching for is squarely within and before you—that it is merely being glossed over. Most seekers think that "enlightenment" will make an appearance or descend upon them at some future date, and hopefully soon! But "it" has already happened! Your thinking and notions about it (that it is time and action-depend, that it is rapturous, that it has to be maintained, that it propels you into some catatonic state, etc) are causing you to be perpetually behind the curve on awareness's recognition. All that's needed is an easy alertness to that which is unmoving and perpetually present.

PURPLE FLOX

I recline on the blue beach under the Sycamore tree. The two-tier bird fountain gurgles nearby. Beyond it, purple flox and "Teddy Bear" sunflowers revel under a brutal sun.

Though the temperature is 97F, it feels like 108-degrees with the humidity. My bottle of once-chilled green tea sits on the wooden circular table before me. "Someone" has no inclination to drink the tea at all. Yet, my body is craving it. Who is overriding what? It would, perhaps, be fodder for an interesting philosophical discussion with someone, but I sit at the table, alone. I'm *always* alone, even when I'm in a room or mall-full of people. My friend, preparing eggplant parmesan (with tofu rather than risotto) peeks from the kitchen door to check on me. She asks, half-jokingly, "Are you going in and out of bliss?" I reply, instantly and sotto voce, "There is no in-and-out of anything." The heat and the mugginess make it toilsome to breathe. Yet, no one is saying, "Forget this, man!" No, this is grace, which is not some heavenly bestowal or uncommon privilege, but the totality of one's Beingness. That is all that is happening right now, under the green light of the sycamore—unbridled grace. You cannot ask or appeal to it, only see that it is here, in this sweltering shade and silence.

PROMENADE

Creativity flowers from stillness, not torment and anguish. It only *appears* to occur when conflict arises. For when there is a momentary cessation in the turmoil, inventiveness flows.

Neither does depravation foster creativity. So go where you are most creative, whether it is a coffee shop, a walk, the kitchen table, your desk, or the shower! Or you may be like this writer: Creativity emerges in all of those places! As for walking, some studies show that as little 10 minutes of daily walking can spur artistry and innovation. Beethoven's productivity was higher during the warm months because he, a renowned walker, could comfortably get out and about during that time. Other prominent walkers included composer Peter Tchaikovsky, poet Wallace Stevens, and the psychotherapists Sigmund Freud and Carl Jung. So take note of where and how your most penetrating ideas happen. There will be times, of course, when you don't want to think about your project at all, which is perfectly fine—even commendable! For this allows you to come back to it with freshness and zeal. With true creativity, you are working hard, but there is a sustained joy within it.

IT'S A GIFT

Presence is always available to you. Never, for even a millisecond, are you not this eternal field of awareness.

Your own true Self has already been conferred upon you. So there is nothing to attain, stabilize, or merge with. When you recognize that what you are—right now!—is your actuality, Self-knowing spontaneously occurs. Yet, it never really happens! Yes, there is a sudden manifestation of unflustered peace and spaciousness; but it doesn't emerge into being. There is not even any shift in perspective! You merely realize that the peace and expansiveness are a gratuity that has already been bestowed upon your body and mind. Your attention and energy had simply elsewhere—on the seeking, the experiences, the journeys, and the supposedly "enlightened" gurus and life coaches. So you have been lost, for years and decades really, led astray by your own all-important deeds and exploits. But none was needed. Not a single one.

INTUITION

That hunch you have about Self-knowledge (i.e., its ease and accessibility) is a priceless one. So be alert to it when it arises. It does so more often than you realize.

Didn't you feel an inner rightness about nonduality? Didn't you experience a smidgen of apprehension when you were in the faraway presence of some showy guru? Weren't there concerns about the huge amount of money you paid for some expensive retreat or costly mantra? Weren't you discomforted when some teacher would not answer your question about whether he or she was self-realized or not? Didn't you have subtle reservations every time "spiritual master" said that you needed to "deepen" your practice? All of those are instances in which your heart was leading the way. Attend to it always.

U.G.

U.G. Krishnamurti once quietly uttered, "I am in that state. Right now, I am in that state." How simple and potent that. He continued to talk about other things, but those two sentences were both calm declarations and very powerful pointers.

Though he was referring to himself, he was speaking about you, as well—for he was not one to dwell upon himself for long (though that would have been welcomed here, given his travels, perceptivity, and caustic wittiness). You yourself are currently in that state and *are* that state. Your own true Self is there for the seeing. That was what U.G. was constantly attempting to do: To point the finger back at your own awareness. I often bristled at his insults and the demoralizing hopelessness that he rained down upon spiritual seekers. I understand what he was doing (making clear that seeking *is* hopeless because you are searching for what you already have; and even worse, your search involves thought, and thus the mind; so you end up going around mindless circles). But why the animus? If you offer mostly that, along with the supposed futility of self-knowing, then most seekers will be completely disheartened. I suspect that U.G. took no pleasure in his exasperation and lack of encouragement. It was simply another way of pointing to the sheer futility of practices and meditation as gateways to self-awakening.

THE NEARNESS OF THAT

Most gurus give seekers what they want: Methods, mantras, and modus operandi.

True teachers, however, provide seekers with what they didn't know they needed, whether it is through phone conversations, person-to-person talks, Skype discussions, or even emails. The teacher's pointers, explanations, and detailed clarifications help to keep the person on track with his or her insights and introspections. Occasionally, the spiritual mentor's pointing results in the seeker's direct recognition of her fundamental state. She will be astonished by her ease of seeing, with the unforeseen immediacy of presence. But there is no nearness whatsoever. For she has discovered that she is That! And that is the astonishment of it all, the great good news that perpetually proffers itself.

BEING ORIGINAL

C.S. Lewis tells us that "Even in literature and art, no man who bothers about originality will ever be original; whereas if you simply try to tell the truth (without caring twopence how often it has been told before) you will, nine times out of time, become original without ever having noticed it. Give up yourself, and you will find yourself."

When you speak directly from presence, originality is inherent within your words, phrasing, and articulation. Thus anything you create is likely to be awash with archetypal boldness and ingenuity. You have only to witness the groundbreaking words and dialogues of Nisargadatta Maharaj, H.W.L. Poonja ("Papaji"), and U.G. Krishnamurti to see the clear evidence of this. Ditto "Sailor" Bob Adamson in our own time. Those luminous guides didn't attempt to be original. Originally flowed from them, making their words, phrasing, and expressions direct pointers to the Truth. Turn to any page and presence will be found, vibrant and revelatory.

DAYBREAK

I write while sitting on a blue bench beneath a 20-year old sycamore. The early morning sun filters through the broad, verdant leaves. Hushed breezes caress my hair and face.

It's the backyard of a friend's house, and I'm relishing my second cup of Trader Joe's Kauai Whole Bean coffee. A dog barks, lightly and in the distance, then stops. It is precisely 61F now. But the temperature will reach 99F by early afternoon. Who could predict that here in the cool and the shade—with the enlivening gushes from the orbed birdbath—that the day would be scorching at some later hour? I love the varying temperatures, and even the promised heat to come. That's just a facet of the personality within this particular body/mind. That personality is such a tiny aspect of the unchanging light of perfection, which is the essence of each of us. The personality, of course, is really a non-factor in your identity. Ditto your gender, profession, or national origin. Indeed, how could any of these be akin to your fundamental Self? Even the word is just a pointer to what you are right now. So what is the *whatness* that is being pointed to here? Stay with the question, with curiosity and earnestness, if you are drawn to do so. Keep things simple and inviting. Again, what is the *whatness* that is being pointed to at this very moment? Only you can answer that question.

THE SWEETEST MUSIC

When flutists and wind players perform, they aren't attempting to blow large amounts of air into their instruments. For the air is already there. The musicians are merely (and skillfully!) vibrating the ether to create the exquisite sounds that we hear.

Likewise, self-knowing isn't about creating or attaining anything new. The "air" is already there. Awareness is fully present. All that is missing is your recognition of it! You can easily go a lifetime without noticing that fact. When you seek it with thought, devotion, or action, you miss it entirely because your focus is on the above endeavors. You are completely overlooking the thing for which you are searching! Further, methods and practices only strengthen the ego, not dissipate it, because an assumed person or individual is in the role of the Doer. If, however, you were to recognize or understand that there is a subtle presence within you that both timeless and unmoving, your attention and curiosity are more likely to go to what and where that subtlety is. Then there is neither a search nor a searcher—just That which always was and always will be.

REGIMEN

Writing is what I do in the morning. I don't think any more about it than I do about the coffee I make. Whether it's book revisions or blog postings, I get up (around 4:00am) and begin.

Part of the essence of creativity is a routine. It seems to foster originality, where thoughts and thinking are anything but routine. Indeed, they are at once clear, elegant, direct, and pause-worthy, when the "flow" is there. The reader is made a more reflective or contemplative by perusing them, though he or she may be at a lost how that is happening. No matter. For when equanimity is suddenly and momentarily present, there won't be a "person" to experience it. This applies to the creator of the work, as well. There is just this heartfelt contentment in your craft, art, or practice. The occasional sense-of-self is not noticed in the least.

UNBOUNDED

True creativity doesn't take you out of your comfort zone—it deepens it. It indubitably shows that your essence (from which creativity arises) is boundless and salubrious.

Doesn't spontaneity, serenity, and penetrating insights generally have an intuitive "rightness" to them? Don't they appear to be the product of something vast, nameless, and numinous? That inherent suitability is one of the hallmarks of someone having chosen well when it comes to his or her work, craft, or even hobby! It's like you have followed your fascination, and you are naturally and uniquely yourself. Yes, the work may be intense or exhausting at times, but the hours appear to hurtle by; you move pass mistakes without blame or regret. Then you find oneself naturally returning to your desk or easel the very next day, with neither dread nor burnout.

THE IMAGINED "I"

In a contemporary book on meditation and mindfulness, I read how the meditator, while sitting, should "remain open and receptive to all that arises." Why? And to what purpose?

All that arises are experiences, other thoughts, memories, and various sensations. How is their appearing and disappearing going to take you to Truth? And who exactly is attempting to stay open and responsive—not to mention awake!? Experiences, however grand or transcending, cannot transport you to your natural state; neither can the imagined "me," which is just another appearance. You are awareness, the immeasurableness in which experiences occur. Your focus should be there and not on the thoughts and adventures emanating within it. Your attention is on the wrong thing! Further, why the repeated meditations? Presence, once recognized, need not be sought again. That's part of the so-called understanding: That you categorically never move from being awareness itself.

AMBLING

You love to walk, especially in autumn and winter, when the chill and cold are invigorating. In summer (at least here in the South), the heat and humidity are too formidable for extended treks.

When you walk, you do it briskly, maintaining the same speed over hills and level ground. Your mind is on overdrive, thinking and contemplating with breakneck abandon. Ideas emerge and disappear, emerge and disappear. Some are useful, others are not. You make mental notes of those that are, scrawling them into your smallish black notebook when you're back at your apartment or while sitting in Starbucks or the Barnes & Noble cafe. Creative and literary vibrancy nearly always appear to be there, allowing you to write practically anywhere. And that mental energy even continues into the afternoon and night, refusing to slow itself, though the body is exhausted and wants to do nothing but be still. You are alert to how this particular body/brain/personality are structured, which readily allows you to utilize them toward their capacity.

AN END TO SORROW?

Is self-realization an end to sorrow? No. As long as you are existing with your body and brain, emotions are going to burgeon. They are part of your temperament and neural functioning. You are not an automaton.

With Self-knowing, though, comes the recognition that all emotions are fleeting—that by their very nature they are short-lived, however powerful, beautiful, and heart-tugging they may be. But if they are fleeting, why should there be any long-term attachment to them? And if there is no attachment, there is no prolong sorry. The sage cries just as easily as she laughs; but the feelings and sympathies are of little consequence, just other appearances in life. Nothing is avoided or excessively categorized. So don't be unduly concerned with emotions. If they appear to be normal, and no medical or psychological authority has told you otherwise, live your life as fully as you can. Or rather, see that your life is being *lived*. That is the view from which sorrow takes a back seat.

Hushed Morning

I sit at the table with its powder-blue cloth. It is 65F and completely shaded beneath the towering Sycamore. I turned on the double-tiered water fountain earlier, which is part of this backyard haven at your friend's house. How long have I been out here, scribbling in this black notebook pad? Time appears to scurry these days, as if "life" has been put on *fast forward*. Yet, time is nothing but a concept, one in which I rarely think about. Indeed, I'm always forgetting my age, birthday, years on a job, etc.

This house is less than a mile from where I live. Here, it's quiet, suburban, and teeming with trees. My one-bedroom apartment, however, is on a busy street overlooking a busy shopping area, both of which are perfectly fine. On my days off, my friend asks if I am "coming to the country." I nearly always do and sometimes spends a night at her spacious, kitty-filled home.

One of the first things I do when I come over is to turn the fountain off, drain it, and clean it. It gets green and gunky from algae and bird defecation. Various feathered creatures revel in the dribbling drench, particular the robins, blue jays, cardinals, and chickadees. But again, they defecate in the very water that they are drinking and bathing in. One day, some bird just might have the inclination not to do discharge its feces into the liquid. From that point on, it will either come to the fountain early, to enjoy the water at its freshest, or just to bathe in it and drink somewhere else. Just by these actions, the bird will stand aloof from others, not because it is better bird, but it is more aware, more watchful, more knowledgeable. This story is apropos to us humans, as well. Why give credence to every thought and emotion we have? Why wallow in pools of tempestuous and psychological excrement? Why do we feel it is necessary? Are there *any* circumstances under which it would be a wholesome thing? No. We needn't do that at all. And you would be a far, far better bird for it.

THOUGHTS AND THE THINKER

Thoughts come first and then the thinker. But here's the thing: The thinker is just an elaborate figment, one that has its day-to-day uses, but is merely a notion and idea kept alive by memory.

When you have the thought, "I am a spiritual person," the thought is real (as far appearances go), but the "spiritual person" is not. There is a body/mind entity there (that is also an appearance), and therefore thoughts are occurring. There is no defined entity deliberately choosing and ordering them. Or to put it another way: There is an enormously complex neurological functions going on here, but no free will. Yes, you can decide not to cross the street, but from where did the thought arise? It doesn't come from an autonomous person; but rather, from your brain, which gives information and directives by way of your body's responses to the environment. That said, your body and neural network are unlike any others' in the world. Yet, fundamentally, every person is this single Intelligence that is without beginning or end.

Yet Another Thing

To be truly creative, you have to be ruthless—not only about your hours at your desk (that happens naturally here), but about time spent elsewhere.

I happen to write best in the mornings, from 4:00am to noon (stopping at 6:00am on my workdays). It is only after those hours that I have time for other matters, which means I have to be *very* selective about what they are. I will, for example, have to decline an invitation to speak at a group or conference because it is not on one of my off-days at work. Since I have only two days off per week, they swell with activity, e.g., phone consultations, blog postings, replying to emails, laundry, grocery shopping, catching the bus to and from the library for books and DVDs, etc. I am organized, but not unnecessarily so. Such a balance allows for both productivity and spontaneity. For some people, their schedules are all-consuming. They actually define the people themselves! Productivity and insights then suffer. Why? Because they are too concerned about their calendar rather than about their work or craft. You "practice" creativity by being creative, by fully engaging in that which you love. No prep work or exercises are at all necessary. That's the simple truth of it.

NO CHANGE

At 89, Nobel-prize-winning writer Doris Lessing wrote, "Don't imagine you'll have it [creativity] forever. Use it while you've got it because it'll go; it's sliding away like water down a plug hole."

I strongly disagree. One's creative juices do not have to fade, fizzle, or trickle away. If your physical self is kept in reasonably good shape, the brain and heart will be all the better for it. What happens, I suspect, is that some people lose the *energy* to create by their sedentary ways, unhealthy eating, and lack of mindful activity (reading, talking, exploring the Web, etc). If the person's stamina, vibrancy, and enjoyment are there, creativity will be too, in all likelihood. There are numerous people to support this: Raymond Chandler didn't start to write earnestly until he was 44; Paul Cezanne didn't complete his acclaimed "Le Grandes Baigneuses" until he was 66; Goethe completed *Faust* when he was over 80; Pablo Casals continued to do concert tours at 88; Henri Matisse produced six major art books between age 75 and 80; Michelangelo was appointed chief architect of St. Peter's in Rome when he was 71; and Mother Teresa and the painter Grandma Moses didn't creatively flourish until in their later years.

Guest Room

Apart from sex and Publix's Black and White cookies, there are no real desires here. There are the requisites wants for food, clothing, and shelter; but those are necessities in life, not desires. And those necessities need not be elaborate or costly for this body/mind/personality.

There are no impulses for exotic travel, hordes of books, expensive dinners, stylish clothes, etc. Even my television set isn't connected: I use it to watch DVDs from the library and Redbox. I rarely buy a book, though I will occasionally buy a *New York Times* or *Wall Street Journal* if they have stories in them that interest me. But I haven't bought a spiritual book since 2007, the year in which this understanding occurred. I have examined works from time to time, mainly when I've come across them in a bookstore. After a minute or two, I'll put the book back on the shelf, seeing neither the substance nor the appeal in it. I did, however, recently had the chance to peruse *Pointers from Nisargadatta Maharaj*, which I had not had an opportunity to examine before. I read it, from cover to cover, in Washington, D.C. (there to do a talk) while snug on a bed in a book-filled guest room. Midwinter sleet clicked heavily against octagonal, second-story windows. Rarely have I been happier.

SLEEPLESS IN COLUMBIA

I've long suffered from insomnia. I hesitate to use the word "suffer," given the grievous ailments that some people have. Still, not being able to go to sleep at night is a condition that I wouldn't want anyone to have to persistently experience.

Along with being middle-age (a time when the body produces far less melatonin, a hormone that helps regulate sleep), my insomnia appears to come from an overactive brain—which often overrides my exhausted physical body after work. Yet, my restlessness abounds with stellar company. A few of my fellow insomniacs include, Mark Twain, Vladimir Nabokov, George Gershwin, Charles Dickens, Marcel Proust, Glenn Gould, Tom Brokaw, Jimi Hendrix, and Sandra Bullock. Ambien (Zolpidem) is the only thing that works for this body/mind. I've tried practically every homeopathic, naturopathic, Ayurvedic, and over-the-counter product for my sleeplessness, and none of them were worked—not a single one. Interestingly, researchers and scientists are not sure exactly why Ambien is as effective; but that appears to be the case with all things extraordinary, from electricity and Ibuprofen to lightening bugs and personal consciousness. We don't have a full understanding of how they operate, but they do. And we are grateful for their alchemy.

PRECISELY THAT

June dawn. High today 95F, with a "real feel" of 106-degrees. I sit on a black bench in my friend's front-yard garden. She has planted more roses—their heads, bright and rufous—next to the solar-powered fountain, which is a miniature oasis for the birds when the afternoon sun moves mercilessly to this south side of the house.

I have both coffee and a book on the bench; however, I hardly ever get around to reading anything when I sit like this in the early morning hours. After a while, I'll put the book down, sip my coffee, and simply savor quiet. White, rippled clouds soar high above. There is even a plane now, having left our local airport heading and probably heading to Charlotte, Washington, D.C., or New York. I have flown at this hour numerous times. Now there is no desire to go anywhere at all.

A woman passes by with her dog. She smiles and speaks, as do I. Then I return to the sitting, not even drinking my coffee. There is no annoyance when I speak to these early morning walkers, no "coming out" of any state, and no any "reentering" one. Even when speaking, spaciousness is there. Then, very naturally, I return to the half-closed eyes and stillness. Nisargadatta once said that he is always meeting seekers who are restless, anxious, and suffering; rare is it he said that he meets someone who is actually content. But I am precisely that.

YOU ARE WHAT YOU ARE RIGHT NOW

Nonduality requires your attention, not your beliefs, opinions, or theories. It doesn't care in the slightest whether you are a Hindu, atheist, or evangelical Christian.

And why should it? Nonduality is an ageless teaching that points to the fact that you are one thing only: Awareness itself. You can label it anything you want: God, Brahman, or Goldilocks. Do you think awareness cares? You are what you are right now, and that is an unchanging, immeasurable vastness that makes the universe, with its billion light-year distances and supermassive black holes, appear like a grain of sand, in comparison. The universe is an appearance *within* you! Feel the pause that ensues from that statement. The universe is wholly within you! But you are looking out and being fascinated by that multitude of things, which is fine and has its place. But the wonder is within, and it is there for the seeing. Absolutely nothing is missing. Nothing.

GREAT WORKS

Just as there are geniuses themselves, there are also things of genius. They are things that you cannot imagine the world being without—at least that is my description and interpretation of it. I'm sure that other philosophers, sociologists, and historians have their own assessments of what exactly categorizes great works.

To my mind, such works would include: Google, Paypal, Amazon, Apple computers, brewed Coffee, bottled water, microwave ovens, books (paper and digital), newspapers (paper and digital), Bach's music, WD40, Ziplock freezer bags, Aikido, the Internet, Ibuprofen, DVDs, Dictionaries (paper and digital), cell phones, televisions, Aeron office chairs, remote controls, contact lens, Wi-Fi, hand sanitizers, Smucker's Strawberry Jam, Margaritas, travel-size items, light bulbs, and—perhaps most brilliant of all—Duct tape.

SACRED INTONATIONS

If you are drawn to chant mantras or sacred names, continue to do so. Done in moderation, they do no harm. Just keep in mind is that the names are not the thing itself.

Years down the road, you may start to grow weary (even bored!) with your singing and recitations. Then you may be drawn to investigate that presiding principle by which everything else is known. You must look directly into yourself to know yourself, to discover that principle. It cannot be done by reciting words, songs, or chants. Those things, however beautiful and mesmerizing, are merely appearances; they arise and disappear, come and go. Something, however, is not coming and going in the least, something is continuing to exist in all of its fullness and subtlety. Bring your focus to that and you are free.

6:35AM

You are back on the bench (this one in the front yard) with coffee in hand. Dark, damp wood chips provide a cushiony underfoot, and a pallid picket fence—braced with Chrysanthemums and Knock Out roses—help to keep you cloaked from passersby, who, more often than not, are either young or older women, striving to keep their graceful haleness.

There is a natural response to look up briefly when the women pass, who are occasionally accompanied by their pets or partners. You neither speak nor establish eye contact with the women—returning, instead, to your little black notebook, on which you are writing these words. For the most part, the women radiate boredom, angst, and a disquieting aloneness; whereas I am totally at ease. In no way can this feeling be described. Can you measure the immeasurable? The moment you put presence into words, it becomes something known, an idea, a semblance. Then that is traded about and readily used, making its viral and tweeted rounds. The words or expressions are given a life (of sorts), leaving users in a world of likenesses and supposition, where their innate freedom is entirely missed.

WHY FOLLOW?

A well-known spiritual teacher often advises seekers to, "Follow the movement of sorrow."

Can you end sorrow by following its rising and falling? Can there be a complete ceasing of it after doing just that one thing? No. You can only end sorrow by understanding it. And that understanding comes on multiple levels. One, anything that comes and goes can't possibly be what you fundamentally are—for your essence *must* be something that doesn't alter in the least; Two, once you start to "follow" your sorrow you are establishing a relationship with it, giving it a weight and credibility that it does not have; and three, the follower is imagined also—for it too comes and goes. So how can one notion help another? How is anything ever come of that? You have to understand that all the above is being witnessed anyway—by awareness. Thus, no "follower" or "following" is needed. Indeed, all of those actions are getting in the way! But don't "get out-of-the-way" of sorrow! That would be the constricted-you attempting to resolve things, again, on the conceptual level. Simply know that the answer to all of this is your very own vastness, which is directly within and before you at this very moment. This very moment! See what it is that is not being seen. That recognition, I assure you, could not be any simpler.

A SUDDENESS OF SUNSHINE

What does it feel like, this glorious, nonevent of self-realization? How are the first few moments? No sage has ever talked about that. But given that 99.99% of the world's teachers have not experienced it for themselves, they wouldn't have a clue what to say. They simply want to continue to give seekers the impression that this understanding has happened with them, and that they should be given rapt attention, not to mention hordes of money for what they have discovered, but in fact have not.

With this body/mind, there was an immediate vastness within and before me. Please know that these are only words, and therefore can in no way accurately reflect what I experienced. They are an approximation, at best—pointers to that nondual Existence that we all are. But there it was, a felt and sudden limitlessness. There *could not* have been any movement whatsoever; and yet, there seemed to be a momentary expansion of sorts, like a suddeness of sunshine, a sweeping forth of light and shadow that one sometime espies across prodigious fields of wheat, grain, or tobacco. Again, this could have only appeared to be the case! Awareness Does Not Move. But I innately knew that this was It—the thing sought for all of those years, more than a decade really. Nonetheless, there it had been, right there inside of me and as me, the entire time. I had sought it everywhere—retreats, practices, devotion, and even a brief period of regimented celibacy—but, as it turns out, there was never a moment that I was without it! It was precisely who and what I was. It was as if I had been looking for my eyes the whole time, but my eyes were doing the seeing. How can you see your own eyes? You can't (except within a mirror). All you can do is realize that your eyes are doing the seeing, that you are the Knowingness. And with that recognition, comes the space in which you have always been and will always be—unbridled presence.

REFERENCES

The quote from Nisagardatta at the start of this book is from: Jean Dunn, editor. *Consciousness and the Absolute: The Final Talks of Sri Nisargadatta Maharaj.* Durham, North Carolina: Acorn Press, 1994, p. 71.

The Doris Lessing passage in my essay "No Change" comes from: *The New York Times* / Book Section. May 12, 2008. "Nobel Regrets for Doris Lessing," by Lawrence Van Gelder

The C.S. Lewis quote in the essay "Being Original" is from book: Dinty W. Moore. *The mindful Writer: Noble Truths About Writing.* Somerville, Massachusetts: Wisdom Publications, 2012, page 40